MAJOR ARCANA
A JOURNEY THROUGH LIFE

William Hall

This is a work of fiction. Names, characters, businesses, places, events and incidents are either the products of the author's imagination or used in a fictitious manner. Any resemblance to actual persons, living or dead, or actual events is purely coincidental.

CONTENTS

INTRODUCTION

This book represents thirteen years of study and meditation on the Tarot and its meanings. This is my personal interpretation filtered by the circumstances of my life at the time when I was first introduced to the Tarot. I could not find all of the answers for what I have experienced nor a proper way to sort, organize and file my experiences on just the Bible alone. Not downing the Bible at all; it's a fabulous text, and one of the best books written of all time if you take the emotion and fear out of it and read for content. I searched and searched for answers, mostly in the area of dealing with different sorts of relationships. Some people I could handle, some I couldn't handle, some seemed to hate me for no reason, when working together is clearly the best option. Sometimes my presence would move people to different reactions before I even spoke a word.

You can pick up the psychology textbook, and it still can only give you a logical view of emotions (an oxymoron in itself). The Bible would have you label everyone that disagrees with you as "demon-possessed", and that's just always not the case.

I found out a big part of Life refuses to be captured in a book. You can only get it by living it, going out having a wide variety of experiences, talking to different types of people. Seeing what their reaction is to you. If it's not in line with what you expected, why? What are other people's take on what they witnessed? I still am not done (I don't think you can ever be done with growing, learning and processing Life), but when I came across the cards, things jumped out at me in a way that said "there's something to be penetrated here, and you just may come back with the right set of *feelings* about the world and myself. I started to journal my thoughts as I would see different events happen that related to a particular card I had seen, and this is the summary of the journals of my journey.

Enjoy!!!
!

I

THE FOOL

Beginning the journey through the pathways of the mind, the Fool is like a newborn hatched chick. He (or she) *thinks* they know everything about everything, and haven't realized they know nothing about their surroundings. They haven't even learned the meaning of "When in Rome, do as the Romans do". They don't even realize they're in Rome. They are also completely oblivious to the fact there is an inner road to travel also. Ignorance is bliss in this case, even though he's about to fall off a cliff as depicted in the card.

In the real world, you have so many different conditions, personal ties, and structures to navigate that don't necessarily reward based on performance. You may just run into cultures that reward based on mediocrity, or as long as none break out of the pack. After some time, you should start making the connections that none of this is by accident, and that you only see so many responses from others that you should be able to start guessing who is good, bad and/or indifferent.

The Fool is not foolish in his own eyes, but his perspective is small and self-centered. The fool doesn't even take into account all of the different dynamics that directly affected their current situation. Being the Fool may not always necessarily have to have a negative connotation. It could be related to a newborn baby, or a toddler just learning to walk and talk. They are completely helpless and defenseless to the intentions of older people in their world.

But as I will attempt to illustrate, The Fool journeys through the arcana to arrive at The World (matured and crowned in wisdom), but yet has gone nowhere physically, even though physical travel may be part of the lesson. The Fool is something like a seed that hasn't even been planted, but from this one seed, a forest might be spawned.

"I could have freed a thousand more slaves if they knew they were slaves" – **Harriet Tubman**

II

THE MAGICIAN

The Fool finally realizes there's a path to be followed, or a reason behind events that happen in his/her Life greater than pure coincidence and dumb luck. The Fool should also realize they have just been standing still in a fixed frame of mind. Either or, something intuitive has been urging them to progress through the things of Life that can't be learned in a book. The Fool begins gathering the tools which includes all the elements to create infinity in front of him (or her). But it takes the missing fifth element to make them work--the spirit of man (or woman). The Magician finds himself, we all find ourselves, about to start on a journey in the inner Life; inner world.

I see The Fool strongly linked to The Devil and The Chariot. The Chariot represents a stage of open conflict from outside sources since none of us live on an island. We do have to factor in jealousy and envy when dealing with outside sources; if we go as far as to believe in demonic attacks directly or through people. As with the story of Cain and Abel, all of these are motivated in the simple jealousy that one builds something with respect to Spirit and Divinity and is therefore blessed. The other builds without respect to Spirit and Divinity. The creation looks good and tempting on the outside but like junk food, is garbage once consumed. Its work always crumbles at a crucial point like The Tower, being devoid of respect to Spirit and Divinity. Then it wants to attack those who do build and create, believing the Divine has shown them "more" favor when in fact, the opposite is true. Abel reached out to the Divine, Cain did not. Cain felt his works were not blessed, and then exacts a revenge on Abel.

Envious people are really looking for a blessing they believe they did not get while at the same time, they refuse to look within. They want to stress everyone around them. They draw a little energy from the attention and anger of others, but are able draw more from themselves. But like most, the beginnings of the journey are uncomfortable. People run from the discomfort as soon as the journey begins to look like work they begin to blame and deflect. An example can be found in Bruce Lee. One of the best, most focused, wisest individuals and martial artists to walk the face of the Earth was always humble in Spirit. Which is why I believe he was able to do the things he was able to do with a relatively small body and physique, yet was the most powerful man in the room anywhere he went. He was able to play ping pong with nunchuks, use the three-inch punch, and the list goes on of his power.

Metaphorically, Life is four elements. Earth, in electricity (a form of Fire), basic wiring says every circuit demands a "ground" to be complete. In other words, Fire cannot move without being connected to the Earth. Let's look at how a car works. You turn the ignition, which sends a spark; gasoline is squirted into a combustion chamber, drawing in Air, to create Fire. The ignition (electric current) needs a "ground" (Earth) in order to complete its circuit. Without connection to the *ground*, no energy can be transferred. Once all of these processes are complete, the car still needs a cooling system (Water) to stop the Fire element from getting out of control. But in order for any of this to come together, that missing, invisible element is the unseen mind of the engineer who brought all the different elements together in a certain order so that we can travel faster and further without thinking about the what or why.

III

THE FAMILY

The High Priestess, The Empress, The Emperor, The Hierophant

For the following four cards, for the purposes of the book, I am grouping them all together, as in my interpretation, what you are looking at here is an analysis of family dynamics we all have to sort out. The more I thought about them and meditated on the subject, I see these four running together as the "train tracks" of your Life. Separating them in this case would be redundant.

The High Priestess:

Is the grandmother's influence that sets the emotional undercurrent of how family will be run emotionally (or clash). At some point, we have to break away from that too, taking what's good and leaving behind what's bad. It's beautiful on one hand to be able to look back at Grandma's wisdom accumulated over the years, but at the same time, Grandma also could be stuck in negative feelings and/or negative ways of doing things. Life does march on, for example, at 35, I then had to be humble enough to let the 18-19 year-olds show me how to work a smartphone.

This card (in addition to the Empress) reminds us at some point; we will have to discard feelings from the past and move forward, or be thought crazy.

We look to our grandmother's as the High Priestesses of the family, providing everyone with spiritual guidance. But good spiritual guidance also knows, no matter how painful, everyone has to find their own way for themselves. Even if you beat a person into a perfect Life, it still wouldn't be authentic, and then you end up with Michael Jackson. And it would only be perfect outwardly, as the changes are not inspired from within. I know I would love to be able to spare my son from any pain that might come his way. However, this is the only thing that will inspire authentic growth in his life.

Grandmothers always seem to have the answer to everything emotional, because by that time, they've already "been there, done that". But there comes a time when we have to rely on our own spiritual compass, and that the only way we can appropriately transition into the next role(s).

In my personal life, I went through a major conflict with my grandmother at the point where, because I began to find out what reliably worked for *me*, I became the villain of all her stories. Once I stopped adhering to what she said as dogma, and began to find out she wasn't right about everything all the time, and began acting on the new information, getting the right outcomes, she then chose to "punish" and "discipline" me back into ways that don't work anymore. Even now, I am still a pariah in her and her minion's eyesight for discovering what works for me and what doesn't.

At any rate, the overall moral to learn in my opinion is accepting family influence, discovering yourself inside of family influence, and then claiming yourself for yourself so that you may provide better guidance to the following generations.

The Empress:

The Empress is a call to look at your relationship with your mother, and she influenced the way you feel and interact in relationships. The High Priestess, in the grandmother role, is more of a pace setting influence, while the Empress, relating to mother, holds a direct view into how you directly learned to *feel* about your world. Femininity stems out of the right side of the brain, is creative and off-kilter at times, but Life is creative and off-kilter *all* the time. The challenge is how do you respond? How do you nurture and give love? As a man, what are your expectations of women, especially in love? As a woman, what relationships do you gravitate towards? How do you decide what men will be friends and which will become lovers? The tone for all of these questions are most likely going to stem out of how you relate to your mother. Are you always looking for someone to hate, or someone to blame? If that's the case, you may want to take a look back and see did your mother look to someone to hate and someone to blame. Was your mother looking for someone to "rescue" her from Life, or from herself? Mothers are our first teachers, uniquely laying down the blueprint of each and every one of our life choices. For this card, this is why I ask you to do more questioning and observing than any other; the roots here were grown before you came out of her womb. How well did your mother shield you from the ugly things life has to offer, too, until you were emotionally prepared to cope? Did your mother create a harmonious environment to grow up in or a disharmonious environment? What did she cherish the most? Was it love, family, money, status? Perfection is too big a cross to place on anyone's shoulders.

The Emperor:

The Emperor would have you take a look at your father or father figure in Life. The male principle in our lives that guides us firmly, sternly, but can also go overboard turning abusive, or in some cases absent. Hopefully you had a good father or father figure that laid down "ground rules" of behavior and conduct as you were growing up and forming your personality. Hopefully, he guided with wisdom, love and good judgment. Hopefully, he taught you character growing up, a trait that is slowly dying out. When you mention the word "character", most people don't really even know what you're talking about these days, until they've had to deal with some people of bad character. I could give you a dictionary definition of "character", but that would serve no purpose. Instead, I will give you mine, learned from years of experience. Character is defined as (for my purposes), questioning yourself and others with the following question: If you knew you could get away with a certain crime or betrayal without blame, but someone would be hurt over it, would you? The reason I say the dictionary definition is no good here is that you can't truly define this until you're *living* the situation. Maybe it's calling in sick from work, but you know they depend on you. Maybe it's an opportunity to cheat on your spouse with someone who looks scrumptious, or an old lover who knows how to push your buttons. Maybe it's a tight football game, you just took a hit that shook you up, you want to sit down, but you know your team needs you for at least one more play. Michael Jordan scoring 38 points sick with stomach flu in the 1997 Playoffs against Utah, Isaiah Thomas in the 1988 Playoffs scoring 41 points against the Showtime Lakers on a severely sprained ankle, Kirk Gibson coming off the bench nursing an injury that kept him out of the game, to hit the game winning homerun in the 1988 World Series, facing Dennis Eckersley, the most dominant reliever at the time.

As a man, you will eventually also grow to become The Emperor to your children or subordinates in the work place. It's up to us to correct the mistakes made by our Emperor, as well as to identify and harness any good life lessons that could be drawn from him.

If Dad was absent (in many people's case), there's most likely some healing that needs to be done in the area of handling rejection. A number of people deal with a vague rage or being overly suspicious of strangers to the point they are pushed away because they have not found how to deal with an absent father figure. You may tend to dwell on bitterness and a perceived hatred by others. At some point, you have to accept yourself, that you are here, and you are alright so as long as you are not harming anyone else (including turning the hatred in on yourself).

The Hierophant:

Grandfathers set the tone of family order, religious views and traditions. No one ever questions "Grandpa" when he speaks; you just do things without question because that's the way he says they are done. The first thing that jumped out at me when I first saw the Hierophant card was an image of the Pope. The Pope quietly and from long range, manages every Catholic household in a grandfatherly sort of way. He may not be seen but he is felt.

Becoming your own Pope is the goal. Depending on your environment, sure it's gonna tick some people off that you are no longer accepting their world view. Break away from adhering to any religious dogma unless it makes sense to you. And sometimes, at the same time, religious dogmas are right. I will always say the Bible (Basic Instructions Before Leaving Earth) is full of wisdom, but don't kill me when I point out it is also full of contradiction, been re-written (I believe the most popular version, the King James) has been copied over 26 times, from the original Aramaic, to Hebrew, to Greek (the Vulgate), Latin, Old English, Middle English, and several rewrites in modern English.

This will strike a nerve with most people, even though I got that information directly from Catholic school. A huge number or grown, financially successful people are still afraid to challenge what they have been told to believe by parents/authority figures. Or on the flipside, have serious problems with anyone that can stand and challenge their perceptions about people, life and reality.

It could be our own cognitive dissonance we need to get past. In other words, we may have gone through Life and up to a certain point, we believed something really random, like all tomatoes are evil and out to get you. Then you get sick and the doctor says you need to eat tomatoes to correct some imbalance in your health system. Do you choose to change your cognitive dissonance, remain ill and die or allow your personal Pope to change so that you can be healthy? You don't know, you just may end up healthier than ever!

It's like watching FOX News versus MSNBC. Fox is obviously slanted to a conservative point of view, while MSNBC is slanted to a liberal point of view. Both are right at times, both are also wrong. But if you are in a staunchly FOX News crowd (or vice versa), the slant becomes a religion you dare not cross. For example, FOX News would have you believe all minorities are untrainable, uneducated scum, sucking America's life blood, but will not debate Cornell West. What they will do is pander to an Allen West or Larry Elder, in other words, minorities that hold the same view points against minorities (as a result of self-hate or a fat payday). Somewhat like Hitler. I wonder do his followers who worship him realize he is one of the people they should be exterminating according to his own doctrine(s)? Cognitive dissonance at its finest!

Conclusion:

Depending on how you personally manage these four areas will determine how you manage the intangibles in Life. We can all set a plan to go from 1st grade straight through to the White House. You can have 10 times the drive of Hercules, but without knowing how to manage the various relationships you will encounter in the world, you could find yourself homeless, working a gas station register all your life (that was something my 7th grade teacher used to scare the class with–"if you do bad on your assignments, you'll end up working at a gas station for the rest of your life"). And that is no knock to people that, maybe were they originated from, the may have had to struggle 10 times as hard as my struggle to even get to work at a gas station in America. My hat is off to them; they've seen things I could never imagine, and still managed to persevere.

IV

THE LOVERS

Fortunately, (or unfortunately), it takes two to make the world go round. I know we'd all like to be one-man (or woman) armies, and we are all feeling more and more generally disgusted with the current state of affairs. I have no answers, all I can say is that things weren't always the way they are now. Hopefully, they will improve as you can observe everything must operate in a cycle. Nothing natural operates in a purely straight line. If you see a straight line, you are either looking at something man-made or you are looking at a very small part of something incredibly large.

Let's take a quick dip into the concept of opposites. Light and dark, positive and negative, hot and cold, up and down, should I continue? We are presented with two polar opposites, and the challenge is to recognize they are just two ends of the same spectrum. Sunday and Monday have opposite ends of the calendar every week, but yet Sunday walks you right into Monday. Even if you don't want to believe the connections, they believe in you and cannot be avoided. I once heard that a surgeon and a mass murderer have the same psychological profile. Both have a desire to cut into to people bodies; one uses it for good, the other uses it for pain and evil. And here's an old street truism to chew on: Good preachers were better pimps...

If you take The Lovers as the awakening of puberty, the natural state of growth is that a young man and young woman desire to couple off, go their own way and make their own family. A cycle is repeated, two cycles merge into one, and at the top of the card, all are being led and connected by a Divine hand.

Everyone seems to be searching for their soul mate at some point in Life after they played the games and bumped their head enough times to know what they don't want in their Life. Is it truly possible some lovers were just meant to be? Deep down, we'd all like to believe that, but does it ever happen? What about a lover you coincidentally run into in different locations and at different times? Is that the hand of God operating? Is it the Devil in operation when we come out of a relationship worse for wear? In every bad relationship, was there some red flag we saw in them, but we *chose* to go forward anyway? At what point do we meet our complement? Is it by allowing the Divine to lead our steps through Life? I still don't have the answer(s) to the above questions, but I have seen enough to know the Divine is real.

V

THE CHARIOT

Fighting energy. War energy. Brute force. Time for battle. Aggression, knowing aggression can also open you up to danger. But some situations will only bend to force. Running full speed just to stay in place. No time to back down or retreat. What has been gained MUST be defended and secured in a military fashion from thieves, rivals. Harnessing opposites to conduct battle. Ruled by Cancer, crabs being known to attack sideways and box their prey in. Pure confidence in yourself is the harness that holds this all together. This stage will demand you to control and master your inner and outer Lives. This represent a stage where maybe you've made your first successes happen, and your success has got the attention of old and new enemies, attracting jealousy and envy because of your success, perceived success or potential success. Maybe your opponent is someone who has a position of authority, they see your ambition and drive, and feel threatened by your progress.

You are making your world move while those around you are stagnating, and they are unhappy about your progress. Think of a point guard (basketball), quarterback (American football) or the pitcher (baseball). At this stage, you are stepping up into a role of warrior and leader. It appears you're going to be given tools to fight the battle (the Sphinxes that pull the chariot. It's apparent in the card they couldn't be any more opposite, but at this time, they require YOU to step into the seat of Divinity to unify their effort! This is the same principle repeated in several cards (The Lovers, The Devil, Judgment, etc.).

Some people are backwards, sideways, Machiavellian – sort of like traffic. In a traffic jam, the new Porsche and the '81 Toyota are equal, both stuck behind the La Cienega bus on the 405 at 4:45. Everybody's not there to do their best, some will try to cut you down for doing you best. Where Life's wisdom comes into play. However, I do believe that the cream must rise to the top, regardless of who tries to hold it down, and the more desirable the cream is, the more obstacles encountered.

At this stage, your presence and progress has made itself known, and speaks loudly even if you do as much as you can to keep your nose to the grindstone, mouth shut and head down. You will have to fight off attackers to maintain your progress, and at the same time, you will have to challenge yourself to rise to the occasion of the confrontation.

VI

STRENGTH

In whatever version you look at, what you see is a woman subduing a lion which could swallow her at any second. She is using her wit and wisdom, grace and seduction even, depending on how you want to view the card. All the time, strength is not overt brute strength. Example: in one aspect, it's bench pressing 400 pounds in the gym (the Chariot), but here, maybe it's the mental strength to get up every morning to build your bench press up from 100 to 125 to 150, so on and so forth until you reach 400.

Referring back to the 90's Michael Jordan Bulls, 4th Quarter execution. You literally had to be up by 12 at halftime to have a chance to win. People see the dunks, the highlights, The Jordan Bulls executed every play to perfection, and the majority was not flashy. They really turned it up a notch MENTALLY and defensively.

Strength is not necessarily in overpowering the opponent, like martial arts. At a certain point, watching advanced martial artists, it's damn near like a dance, and the loser who get they're neck chopped, is the first one to get out of the step or the rhythm of the dance. They both know each other's styles, they both know what's coming next, it's a matter of who has the mental control of self to execute every step without making a mistake.

There is a particular branch of martial arts known as tai sabaki, where the moves are all defensive and evasive. Practitioners take an entire lifetime to master this art, with the end goal being that the practitioners cannot be touched *unless* they want to be touched. Aikido is another martial art based on using the opponent's strength and attacks against them.

Strength can also be exhibited as command or mastery, for example, Greg Maddux. Never really broke 90 mph but was one of the most dominant pitchers of all time. Nothing outstanding, just an excellent command of locating pitches in impossible spots for batters to hit. Along with that, strength was exhibited by a ruthless study of the habits each and every batter he would be facing on a particular day. Strength is not always force; hence a woman was chosen to represent strength of mind and spirit.

VII

THE HERMIT

"Question religion, question it all. Keep asking those questions 'til those questions is solved." – Jay Z, Heaven, Magna Carta

A break away from the Hierophant, High Priestess, Emperor and Empress. Your inner journey to find you. What are you searching for?

Getting alone, even in your own head, to juggle different ideas and observations to draw your own conclusion. This is why the Hermit is alone; it angers the average person when you set off on the journey in your own head space to try to solve your own puzzle. Funny those same people can be repeating an obvious mistake over and over, and will highly resent you for trying to correct them, no matter how gentle you are.

But then I heard it put this way, and it's coincidental that the hermit marches through the darkness with a lantern. Giving some people the truth of a situation is like hitting someone walking on a dark road with a 600 watt flashlight. It will, one, scare the pants off them, and two, hurt their eyes, maybe to the point to which they may react in rage.

I've also heard it put another way, from a Christian pastor who is also a practicing psychologist: The average human being would rather be "right" during an argument than to reconcile the facts and arrive at the truth. This is why some arguments never end. At least one side is unwilling to compromise/admit they may have been in error or overlooked something when they formulated their opinion.

The Hermit wanders the paths of the Tree of Life and may have to also wander the 22 Pathways of Set belonging to the Tree of Death in order to find true light, inner light. When I first heard the term, the "22 Pathways of Set", I was told it was all expressions of wandering around through the nature of evil. Then recently, I heard something completely different; that the true meaning had been hijacked to represent evil, when in the original form, it refers to the different possible pathways neurons in the brain can connect during sleep or meditation. Apparently the ancients had already known each neuron can make 22 possible connections to the surrounding neurons. We learn by being exposed to new information, which taken in, causes the neuron to create different new physical connections than what was previously possible. My mind was blown away. Some of the wisest truisms I've heard in regards to navigating Life have come from drug addicts in the throes of addiction. Only a few people will dare admit some of the best relationship advice can only be gathered from prostitutes and pimps. They are the only ones the can tell you how to deal with your partner's shadow side, and your own, because they live in the shadow side of Life. We have a hard time admitting the shadow side even exists. However, it must be confronted, explored and dealt with before we can be whole.

VIII

THE WHEEL OF FORTUNE

"I said, well Daddy don't you know that things go in cycles" – Q-Tip, A Tribe Called Quest

A picture of the game from a distance. The first thing I want to observe is the letters surrounding the wheel: T A R O. First observation, if you complete this in a circle, then you arrive at T A R O T. Second observation: you can also re-arrange the letters, but in the same order, and get R - O - T - A. Add the T and you get R - O - T - A - T - (E). Life rotates. The Moon rotates around the Earth, the Earth and the other planets rotate around the Sun, and even the Sun rotates around a celestial body in the middle of the galaxy. Clocks rotate. Tires, engines and everything else involved in travel rotates in order to get from a Point "A" to a Point "B". Rotation, rotation, rotation. The seasons rotate in a cycle. Everything in motion is moving in some form of rotation, through cycles so small we can't observe them without a microscope to cycles so large it takes several generations to fully observe.

You have your own personal wheel, and then it engages someone else's wheel, all the time engaging Life's wheels, and I have to have faith it sort of works out something like the gears on a gigantic clock. Some people's gears don't fit together. Some people's have a broken tooth. Some people come together and their gears mesh like hand on glove.

What goes up must come down. Gears have a top position and a bottom position. On a car it's called "top dead center". One is really no different from the other in the grand scheme of things, but when it comes to your personal life and world, it can be uncomfortable and depressing to be at whatever your personal "bottom dead center" is.

Sometimes you get sand stuck in the wheels of your personal tank, like German tanks in the desert in World War II. You have personal cycles of feeling great and not so great linked purely to body biorhythms you have no control over.

The swastika is another form of the wheel of fortune. Keep in mind that the Nazi's adopted it and reversed it, full well knowing the subconscious symbolism. Karma will eventually ground you under unless you allow it to teach you the lessons of how to live a good life.

Now you ask the question why do bad things happen to good people, sometimes just for being at the wrong place at the wrong time? I don't know why that is; all we can hope for is that it's in the Creator's grand plan.

IX

JUSTICE

The figure in Justice also holds their hands in the "As Above, So Below" position, but with a sword and scales. Swords connect to air and the mind (a sharp mind versus a dull mind) and scales connect to Libra. Everything is or eventually will be balanced and accounted for. For every action, there is an equal and opposite reaction. Without the sword, think of a garden that would just grow out of control until it became an untamable jungle. Everything has to have a cut-off point in order to have definition.

What you do with what you are given will be weighed by the divine authority in the invisible world. That being said, it's best to corral your actions and the places of your personality that might be out of control.

Is it "Just Us"? Or "Just Ice"? Athletes know (or should know), using the sports analogy, let's compare and contrast Strength and the Chariot. The Chariot is your "push" power if you have to bench 400 pounds, but Strength can be seen in two ways. One, nobody comes out naturally benching 400; you have to build up to that through strength and consistency of mind. Two, look at anatomy. OK, it's the chest, shoulders and triceps that get developed on the bench, but you must have equally developed biceps and back muscles to bring the weight down under control.

Balance and moderation are key, as with anything that you do. You can over-do anything. You can also drink too much water and kill yourself from that. You need to push for Justice when you see what you can confirm as injustice. At the same time, use judgment before you involve yourself with something you don't know all the details to. Justice asks you to investigate before making a rash decision. One rash decision might cause you to throw yourself into Karma's way.

X

THE HANGED MAN

A good friend said the best thing that ever happened to him in life was breaking his ankle. He couldn't do anything else while he was laid up but focus on his art, and is now making a decent living from it. No athlete likes time-outs, no child likes time-outs, but sometimes regrouping is uncomfortable but necessary. In battle, sometimes retreat is the best option. Mine seemed a bit prolonged, maybe it's because many good things were to develop in that downtime.

I was once told the definition of God's grace is unexpected detours that had you kept going as you planned, like The Fool, you would've ended up in a major car accident or some other kind of tragic event. Life enforced time-outs. I don't like detours; no one does.

The man in the card seems to have a peace of mind. He's been caught in a trap, and now there's nothing he can do about it.

In my opinion, this card should fall in between The Tower and The Star. Being caught in the trap forces him to look up towards the divine. We want to run, run, run all the time. Detours of life are uncomfortable. Some are placed there to test your fortitude and inner strength; some are there to save you from yourself. I'll use a current example I'm delaing with right now as food for thought: As I am writing this, I think I am about to be stood up for a date, partially my fault. The young woman I was hoping to go out with sent me a text last night, and I had a long day, and honestly fell asleep early. I've tried to communicate with her three times today to let her know I was not "blowing her off", but she has not returned my texts. Here is the lesson of The Hanged Man: If I continue to keep attempting to contact her, I look like a stalker. I would also be disrespecting myself to continue to contact someone, that at this point, I have to assume will not be contacting me back. Whether she lost interest on her own, there is someone else she is more interested in or she feels offended, I put my best foot forward with a sincere apology, and now, all I can do is let the chips fall where they may.

But this comes from an accumulation of experiences, good, bad and indifferent, dealing with different types of women, learning their thought processes and having had successes in the past to balance things out. I like this woman enough to consider a relationship, but if she's not on the same accord, I can't force it. Ten years ago, I might have got upset and took it personal, today, I can take things in stride, because I can file it in between success and failure.

XI

DEATH

Sometimes we need to leave certain things alone. As the apostle Paul said, when I was a child, I did childish things, and when I became a man, I put away childish things. Certain phases of Life have to "die" and be left behind in order for a new form of Life to come forward. What if a caterpillar lamented becoming a butterfly? The caterpillar would never know what it could do if it stayed a caterpillar? Either you can fight and wrestle with holding on to an old phase of Life, or you can welcome the falling away. It truly is a scary, frightening process for the old Life to crumble, but the new Life inside you still remains invisible, because the new life is inside you! Think of planting a seed. If you were the seed, wouldn't you be scared as you were being buried? But yet the very same burial will result in an oak tree if you let it. Even for me this is tough.

This process is easier said than done, and uncomfortable. In order to be released from a bad situation in the real estate business, I had to let everything fall away and make an extremely uncomfortable transition into the armed forces, at an advanced age no less. But after a ton of struggle and strife, because I kept a focus and endured, now I am preparing to be accepted at the highest level of nursing, in which I don't know how far I can go with it?

The other alternative is eternal life. You'd be like a vampire, and in almost every vampire story, at some point, they regret not being able to experience death and transit on to a new phase. What if you were the "business" in high school, but then never got out? Really, how would you feel being 26 in high school, the same age as some of your teachers. You cannot stay a child forever; look at death as no more than growing up to a new phase.

XII

TEMPERANCE

The "Temperance" card in the deck is one of the most difficult to penetrate, even if you're fortunate enough to grasp the meaning, you still will never quite know it until you go thru it. I'll start with a story an older guy told me, relating it to Life. He said, hey, I own a '63 Buick that it is simply impossible to blow the engine. The block is solid steel, and in the factory, it was heated to 3500 degrees, while in the worst case scenario, a running engine will only reach about 800 degrees. It's a process that simply has to be lived. It's painful while you're going thru it, but it's a toughening and flaw removal process. One of the other names of the card is "Art", God's art for our lives.

When I passed thru it, it felt horrible, then I had to begin to make conscious effort to "cool myself off" from the tempering. I had to make time to meditate, and force myself to be still and find my center again. With the things I had endured, I had been stretched to my limits and then some, mentally, spiritually, emotionally, physically and financially.

I watched a show on the process of sword making, where the quality of the finished product depends on how long the purchaser is willing to wait. The longer the maker is allowed to heat the steel and then hammer it out, each blow removing the flaws in the material, slowly but surely making a stronger blade.

We all come in to the world as flawed raw beings, the fire being the process that burns up the useless garbage ingrained in our being, into a purified product.

Joel Osteen put it like this: Imagine that every day, $86,400 is put in your bank account. It's yours to spend any way you choose, but you have to invest it or waste it. And if you don't invest wisely, or at least practice, whatever you don't use is taken back out of your bank account. Wouldn't you look at money differently?

This is how time works in your life.

XIII

THE DEVIL

Who or what is the Devil, truly? No one truly knows but only himself and the Creator. He is a real entity to be reckoned with. He is negativity, darkness, everything bad. Some things are inexcusable. I will not go that far to excuse pure evil, having been a victim of it myself.

The epitome of the dark side of each of us, the fantasy world, the fast lane, the one we kind of know will lead us into trouble eventually but it's fun at the time. Like Pleasure Island in Pinocchio. If you look at the card itself, you see a for all intents and purposes, a demonic, horrifying looking creature with a goat's head and horns

The man and the woman chained to his altar both could escape out of the chain at any time, something internal is keeping them there. Superimpose "The Devil" card with "The Lovers". Man, woman, something divine is in between them.

Could we be putting too much emphasis on the hand pointed opposite directions, the "As Above, So Below" pose, and maybe it implies that if you have the Lovers, there has to be a "Devil" between them so to speak that keeps the relationship spicy?

Could the secret of relationships be striking a balance between the Devil and the Lovers?

Could this same identity (every minor suit starts with Two, not One, be what you need to grasp about the Lovers, the Devil, and Judgment?

How do you reconcile both the animal and divine natures? The question you have to present yourself with because man is both. Man is a combination of a lot of different influences. If you want love, does time spent in your animal nature, which is inherently selfish, come back to bite you?

And not just any love, like I've come to grasp one thing: you don't want every woman's love. So the Devil requires you to start being selective in who and what you deal with, and why. With the wisdom of time, trials and tribulations, your circle and who you allow to get close to you has to get tighter, smaller. Is the Devil the mirror that shows you what you need to fix in yourself? Is the Devil the sandpaper and grit that smooths you out, polishes you?

You have to ask a lot of questions here, mainly of yourself. What are your uncomfortable addictions? Sex, drugs, greed? Are you afraid to stand in your Chariot and be the hand of Justice when you know you are witnessing injustice? What is it you are afraid to face? The Devil should help you break out of a "victim" mentality anywhere in your Life where you find the one holding you prisoner is You.

XIV

THE TOWER

The build-up of material wealth and material heights that can all be brought down at moment's notice. The only thing that can never be taken from you is what you have built up internally. The only things you truly own are what you have been educated to. It may not show as external achievement. The only way to get past a loss of material external things is to let them go, understanding that the material achievement/success in and of itself is only temporary anyway. But the prince and princess thrown from the tower our not dead yet. Fallen, yes. In a state of disgrace, yes. Alive, yes. Embarrassed, hurting, yes. Do they have a massive, unpaid clean-up job to do? Yes. The bigger they come, the harder they fall.

You need a shake up every so often when you start giving too much credit to things. Giving too much credit to things can lead you astray, wandering after any and everything that can give you material power. Or that you think can give you material power, to find out it will eventually crumble, it's not eternal.

Once The Tower is removed, only then can one see The Star(s), the true possibility of internal development that can lead you to a true blossoming.

XV

THE STAR

Once the Tower is destroyed (material possessions, fast life, false beliefs, etc.), then the journey can move forward again. Like Nimrod, we invested all our resources into building up an external façade (even though we may have truly believed we were doing the right thing). But even the Bible says a wise man builds his house on bedrock, a foolish man builds his house on sand.

Have you noticed it becomes an awful lot of work to keep up with a lot of material things? They need constant maintenance, wear & tear sets in, some things freeze up if not used regularly, like a car engine. The next thing you know, you've now become a slave to your own possessions. Now that you have these possessions, you have to work an increasing amount of hours in their upkeep, either to do it yourself or pay someone to do it for you. Is faithfully working 60-70 hours a week really living? The next thing you know, you don't even have the time to enjoy these possessions.

It could be the same thing in having a beautiful, wonderful spouse, but now you're working so much you never get to spend time with them, and even the best of relationships wither under benign neglect.

Everything crumbles, or gets blown apart by the divine. We have to grieve over the loss of our time, pride, possessions. But only then, once the Tower is out of the way, the Sun is dark, can we see the Star for the first time. What I mean is only then can you see ALL your possibilities and options.

Charles Barkley made a statement about Dwayne Wade: He's still a great player but he's at a point of his career where he's gonna have to accept he's no longer the best athlete on the court. He's gonna have to adjust his game and start really *thinking* basketball. All the greats had to go through that transition in order to continue on with their careers.

Yes, it's painful and there has to be a grieving process of loss. But then we become students again once we can see ALL of the possibilities.

XVI

THE MOON

The Moon card is representative of the idea of growth, rest, healing that we can't see, can't fathom how it's being done, or if it's happening at all, all powered by Life itself. One, the Moon is the reminder that the Sun is still there. Night has come, but the moon reflects the Sun's light. It reminds us that God is still there. Two, anyone into growing plants can relate to this. Under sunlight, the plant grows, but with out a dark or rest period, the plant will eventually burn up, wither and die. It must be allowed to switch off some time. Growers who manipulate light to force growth also understand they are creating a weaker plant.

There are mysteries that take place under moonlight, the most important being that that is the time we shut down to organize, and let the body rest repair and grow. Of course we don't like it, not just fear of the dark, but being out of God's sight, but deep down we're not aware of that. We don't like it and it's uncomfortable, but new growth is taking place internally that hasn't come out yet. Every strong plant also has to have equally strong but unseen roots.

It's mysterious enough even when the Moon is even there. I remember doing a report on lunar geology, and one of the main points was that where does the Moon come from? The Earth doesn't have the gravity to hold an object the Moon's size, whether the Moon broke off from the Earth or it captured it in passing. But yet it's here.

Don't forget that the Moon has significant effect on the tides and water in general, around the world raising and lowering tides between six and twenty feet everyday. And the human body is also 75% water, almost the same as the Earth. As above, so below.

It takes energy and experience from our dark side, too, in order to develop into that well-rounded person. It's one thing to be orderly, well-regimented and structured, but in the Dark is where the flavor of Life is developed. If you think about it, who are the funniest people? The ones that have been thru some drama, and been able to draw humor out of it, better yet, those who draw humor out of a situation they are in right now. Timing, wisdom, the intangibles of Life that make us into a full human being all come under the Moon. The best example that comes to mind right now is the tragic passing of Robin Williams. Someone so humorous, but it didn't take much to see the dark place that humor emerged from.

The Moon may require you to visit some dark places in Life, or see the disillusionment of what we once thought was a good thing is revealed to be a bad thing with lasting effects that don't go away right away. It may require you to revisit painful memories and emotions, hopefully so that you can see your way out this time, or at least when you have to revisit the dark, you can walk in faith and confidence that everything goes in cycles, and the Sun still also has to rise too.

Move past fear, because every burial is a planting in disguise, if you let it be. So expect a serious blossoming, because serious growth takes place during the period of seasoning. It sucked big time, but in spite of it all, what does not kill you might weaken you for a time, but truly does make one stronger in the end.

XVII

THE SUN

After our trials and tribulations of Life's journey, inner and outer, we know that for every night there must be a day. The Sun represents our re-emergence from the mud, the muck, the drama, the abuse, beat downs, imprisonments, and every other physical, emotional and mental forms of torture we could experience. You also have to keep in mind, as in the Devil, some of the torturous places were our own design on ourselves we don't want to own up to. In the card, you see the Sun hovering and smiling over a child riding a horse, carrying a red blanket. As you penetrate the meaning of the card, I feel the reason the Sun has facial features is that during the phase of being stuck under the Moon, when everything seems hopeless, is maybe the facial features represent finding the Sun *within* yourself as an individual. I believe it comes with a ton of travail, uncomfortable situations, dangerous situations, having to find yourself surrounded by psychosis with no available escape and everything looks hopeless. So maybe you cannot perform a frontal assault and push your way out of the situation. But you can find your way inwards and ignite your own light, your own flame. Look for your own Wheel of Fortune and ignite it. Everyone has some God-given talent they can ignite given enough time and clear space.

That being said, you just might want to avoid situations that become constricting, as they are preventing you from spreading your "wings" to find out what you can really do. Entering this phase, expect that people will start to gravitate to you, you start holding the attention of random people, and you start to be viewed as a life-giver and a wisdom-giver, the same way our Sun holds the Earth and all the planets in order.

XVIII

JUDGMENT

At Judgment, we see a kind of cryptic picture of people in coffins, men, women and children, seeming to be awakened from Death itself by the angel with the trumpet that dominates the top of the picture. What are we to learn from this? The name of the card itself is Judgment, that our actions in our time here on planet Earth will be held accountable. As frustrated and angry and judgmental as I can be about the daily events that go on in our world, traffic, slow drivers, rising food prices, inching closer and closer to World War 3, and the list could go on, possibly it hasn't made itself apparent to you the reader, but the fact that there is something else out there, something supernatural, has made itself apparent in my life over and over again. And I am the biggest skeptic. I believe in nuts, bolts, every action having and equal and opposite reaction. Things I can put my hand on and feel. But a very real presence surrounds us that we cannot see.

For example, someone you were just thinking of happens to call. Your car breaks down, but then you find out later if you had left for your destination on time as planned, you would've ended up in a car wreck. Once, I got one of the worst stomach aches of my life, it forced me to have to go back to sleep. At the time I was working for myself, and time truly is money, so I was not just in pain, but upset at not being able to get to my project site. Then the ache vanishes just as suddenly as it came. Later that day, I found out the place I was en route too was being broken into and vandalized by a hate group, and had I left on time, we would've been face to face; one of us may have killed the other. I could be dead or in jail for the rest of my life.

Another example: I was on my way to hang out and a friend called me, diverting me from my destination. Had I not got that phone call, I would've been caught in the middle of a drug sweep, in which the police had orders to arrest someone that fit my description.

What I'm hoping to discover is that after we have lit our inner Sun, and dealt with the idea that the physical body is vulnerable to attack, but the mind is unlimited, is that when our allotted time is up, even if we died in prison, the angels will call forth, and we will stand before them, ready to account for whatever OUR actions were.

Revelations speaks of trumpets sounding at the time of Christ's return. School is out now, and we are now gonna receive our report cards as to what kind of human beings we were, what we did with what we are given.

XIX

THE WORLD

Finally, we reached the end of the journey at the World, or the Universe. What more is there to do? We've passed all the tests, from being a happy-go-lucky fool, dealing with authority figures in the Hierophant, The High Priestess, The Emperor and the Empress, being in Love, going forward on an unstable platform in the Chariot, beginning a search for the truth as the Hermit, experiencing loss between the Devil, Death and the Tower. The Tower falling to clear the path of vision obscured to the Star (the possibility of what and who we could be), the night of the Moon as a promise the Sun is still there, just not visible, to see our own inner brilliance, being judged by the Spirit, and then handed the keys to the World, or if we fail Judgment, most likely a return to this platform, to experience everything all over again. Once we become the World, who can stop us? But as we should have learned along the way, we must self-check every so often before we have to be shaken back to reality by the hand of the Creator.

When the Fool completes the journey, what does he find? A woman, his opposite in all her glory. Just the other side of the coin, figuratively speaking. I do not believe we actually become a woman, but a union.

Never abandon who you are (The Fool), but acknowledge and accept the opposite polarity (The World). Because they were always unified anyway, so the whole process was to defeat the illusion of separation and opposites. It's the energy in between seen in The Lovers, The Devil and Judgment that makes it all click. Ringed by wisdom and flanked by the same creatures described by Ezekiel in his vision, the bull (ox), the eagle, the man, and the lion.

She floats on her own power, the Sun transformed into a whole person, or you can see what's behind the Wheel of Fortune. Keeping the Spirit portion in mind, never forget you are only co-creating with the Creator. You did not create yourself; therefore you can always be dismantled by the Creator in the blink of an eye no matter how high you *think* you've ascended. We are in the World, but not of the World.

XX

COMPLETING THE SQUARED CIRCLE

On a final note, in my estimation, the Major Arcana illustrates for all of us the stages and houses of Life. So much so that in a sense, someone at stage 20 might sound like a complete idiot to someone at Stage 2 or 3! Learning to let things go so that others may blossom and develop. Again, no better example than the caterpillar that, if you could be in his or her shoes, is probably scared to death at the time of transitioning from caterpillar to butterfly. One of the hardest things to do in Life is trust the process, even when you know the process happens naturally all around you. Our challenge is to master harmonious balance in Life. In some instances, if you don't push for a thing, it won't push to meet you either. For example, yes, Michael Jordan scored 50 and 60 point games, but if you look back at the tape, he had to take about 50-60 shots, too (I don't have the exact number, don't hold me to it, in and of itself the exact number is not important). What is important is that you realize you gotta take a lot of chances in Life in order to be stellar! Or as the street saying goes "Scared money don't make none." We start as Fools, having no idea what it is we are doing, so ignorant and unaware of our surroundings we just wander aimlessly. The Magician appears, wakes us up to the possibilities of what might be, and at least lays the tools out for our success. You got the stages of childhood represented in The High Priestess, The Empress, The Emperor and The Hierophant. Our parents may have been there and gave us the best life possible, they may have been flawed or absent all together. Their job is to shape, nurture and guide us, but after a certain point, we have to establish our own identity separate from them. The Lovers are the next natural point, going thru the stages of "puppy" love, good relationships, bad relationships; relationships that only consist of great sex, relationships that only have great conversation. This could also be the two halves of the brain connecting, or rationalizing your male and female sides within yourself. It's intuitive that before you can truly love someone else, you have to accept and love yourself first. The rub is that you don't know how to do that until you get out there and do it.

The Chariot now brings to the times of Life that you have to fight or be tread under. The Hermit is representative of times of Life when we have to get back and reflect on our prior experiences and what it means to us. Either or, times when there's something we need to know or understand in order to pass on to the next level, but the only way to accomplish it is alone.

The Strength card illustrates for you how you sometimes have to learn to exhibit strength in restraint. Maybe it's being kind when you don't want to. Maybe it's one of those times in Life where like David and Goliath, the strength for David was even to show up to the battle. The Wheel of Fortune is like stepping back to show you everything whirls around in cycles. You could be born in a place, but you don't have to stay in that place. Everything is available, but you got to spin the wheel. You can't score if you don't play. We can all self-direct, but at the same time, can you control the weather? You can't control your heartbeat. Some things you, again, have to let go of, let the chips fall where they may and hope that what goes around comes around. Said to say if you put good deeds and good energy out, that will come back to you too. Justice represents the idea everything has to be balanced at some point, sometimes the balance may have to be achieved by force or authority.

The Hanged Man is about enforced time-outs in Life that you don't really have a choice about. Sometimes Life will grab you by the ankle and up-end you, but maybe the point is so that you can see things from a new perspective, a different point of view. Maybe that hospitalization for exhaustion was necessary before you had a heart attack? Maybe that flat tire delayed you from getting involved in a bad accident? The problem is you won't know what the reason you were delayed until after the fact. Death can be seen as a transition. The fetus has to die to that stage of Life and exit its mother in order to be born into this world. You have to die to an old job to go on to a new better job or business. The Temperance (Art) card is a blending together of previous experiences and skills to weave your own pattern (art form) now. To "temper" something also means making it stronger through a trial by fire. The Devil can represent outer evils, resentments from others who are not growing (or choose not to grow), but it can also be the outer reflection of our own inner demons that need to be dealt with. The Tower is the time when material things are taken away or destroyed (with a bunch of unpaid clean up), but maybe those material things have been taken away because the material was obscuring reality? Of course it's uncomfortable to have your home crumble, but at the same time, doesn't the bird have to destroy its old home in order to learn to fly? The Star is when you can again see the reality of what might be once the Tower is out of the way. The Moon is the phase of disillusionment and grieving over what you thought was real, and it's supposed to be dark and uncomfortable. Representing the times when the wheel has turned and now your parents rely on you. The Sun is the light risen again, and everything is in full blossom, understanding nothing will come *properly* before its time.

Now the light has been cleared and shines from within, instead of looking for light without. Judgment is the time when we all have to give accounting to the Divine. The Egyptians believed all had to stand before the goddess Maat at the time of death. She throws out everything else except the heart, weighing the heart on a scale against a feather. If we can give a solid reconciliation in the presence of the Divine, then we can become The World, The Fool exalted to a small slice of divinity him/herself. Like a game, the true goal is in *finishing* the game, when in this world, my belief and observation is that we get too hung up on collecting coins and trinkets along the way. Then we start looking at the collection of coins and trinkets as a goal and forget to play and finish all levels of the game.

My father used to tell me about a Kung-Fu movie he never could remember the name of, but this was the point: A fighter is in search of a book that supposedly contains the secrets of Life. He goes to a castle and has to fight a different style of fighter at every level. Once he masters their style, then he can go up to the next level, each level getting more and more difficult. Once he finally reaches the top, there's a book on an altar. The fighter opens the book, and sees a mirror. He turns the page and finds another mirror. He keeps turning page after page, and every page is another mirror. In other words, the key is to look at yourself. Maybe you need an adjustment in Life?

www.ingramcontent.com/pod-product-compliance
Lightning Source LLC
LaVergne TN
LVHW051430080426
835508LV00022B/3324